Contents

Page

1. Beginnings 1

2. Tell Me, Auntie! 11

3. Life in Service 20

4. Friends and Companions................. 26

5. Grief Has No Barriers 32

6. Going Home and Making a Living .. 38

7. Love Comes to Aunt Lizzie 46

8. Off to America 53

9. Life After John 60

10. Charlie's Story............................ 66

11. A Big Mistake 72

12. A New Family............................ 75

13. Visiting with Auntie....................... 79

14. Aunt Lizzie's Hat.......................... 85

15. The End Comes............................ 91

    Postscript 96

GREAT AUNT LIZZIE

Winifred Foley

ISIS
LARGE PRINT
Oxford

First published in Great Britain 2002
by ISIS Publishing Ltd

Published in Large Print 2002 by ISIS Publishing Ltd,
7 Centremead, Osney Mead, Oxford OX2 0ES
by arrangement with Winifred Foley

British Library Cataloguing in Publication Data
Foley, Winifred
    Great Aunt Lizzie. – Large print ed.
    (ISIS reminiscence series)
    1. Foley, Winifred – Family
    2. Country life – England –Dean, Forest of
    3. Large type books
    4. Dean, Forest of (England) – Social life and
    customs – 19th century
    5. Dean, Forest of (England) – Social life and
    customs – 20th century
    I. Title
    942.4'13'085'092

ISBN 0–7531–9816–9 (hb)
ISBN 0–7531–9817–7 (pb)

CI 52046605

Printed and bound by Antony Rowe, Chippenham

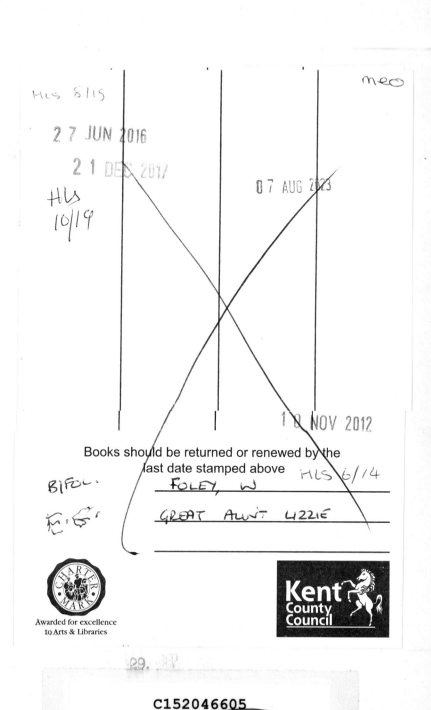

HLS 8/15

meo

2 7 JUN 2016

2 1 DEC 2017

HLS
10/19

0 7 AUG 2023

1 8 NOV 2012

Books should be returned or renewed by the
last date stamped above HLS 6/14

BIFOL:

FOLEY, W

GREAT AUNT LIZZIE

29. SEP

CHAPTER
ONE

Beginnings

It was 1926; I was twelve years old and lived with my miner father, my mother and four other siblings in the cottage we shared with my Great-Aunt Lizzie and which she owned, in a small mining village that straggled up a hillside in the beautiful Forest of Dean.

In the Forest dialect, a head was called "yud" and a clever person was a "long yudded one", a description all the village applied to our Dad. For instance, he repaired an old lathe someone gave him and taught himself how to use it so well that he became the honorary village carpenter and bodger, producing turned chair legs and other wooden objects. With a large old metal container and a pipe bellows, he made a miniature smithy to mend pit-lamps and tools, and do other small metal repairs. He was a keen herbalist and a bee-keeper, so we always had honey. He built a little glass hive in the living-room window for us children to observe what went on in a beehive. Someone gave him an old shotgun and he managed to put it back to working order. To test it, he took a shot at a little bird flying over our garden. It fell to the ground, dead.

Any pleasure Dad got out of his success on his first shot was overshadowed by remorse. "Poor little creature, done no harm to anyone and *I* killed him!" The shotgun disappeared from our lives forever.

A compassionate man with outstanding intelligence, life must have been torture for Dad sometimes. Man's inhumanity to man saddened and angered him. He saw his sisters and daughters go into domestic service, becoming the inhabitants of basements and attics, capped and aproned captives on the lowest rung of the social ladder irrespective of their potential. They carried coal-scuttles filled with the coal dug out from the depths of the earth by their brothers and fathers, to warm their "betters", all for cruelly low wages. The injustice of this made Dad into a Socialist, his outspoken condemnation of local pit-owners leading to victimisation and barring him from work in the Forest mines for seven years, which made our lot worse than most.

With a couple of other erudite miners, he found an outlet for his thoughts and feelings in discussions and arguments round the fireside. Sitting on my usual perch at the end of the big steel fender, I was a fascinated and uncomprehending "little pitcher with big ears". One evening they got onto the subject of the fourth dimension and how matter of any sort began, even putting forward a theory that life was a sophisticated form of thought, not really solid at all. I was about 5 years old, with enough curiosity to be thoroughly puzzled and when Mam came in from our neighbours and hustled me off to bed, I carefully felt the sides of the staircase and the treads under my feet, and was reassured that the world was indeed real and solid.

Mam needed no mental stimulation. Her life was fulfilled with the daily struggle of bringing up her family and giving us treats that cost nothing. When someone gave her an old pushchair, she put the littlest one in and walked us the three miles to the riverside for a picnic — a loaf of bread, a basin with some dripping, and bottles of her home-made dandelion pop. The knife she took with her peeled the swede we nicked from a field on the way, slices of delicious juicy crunchy swede topped our repast. The purse may have been empty in our cottage, but we shared Dad's rich mind and the unstinting love of both parents and dear old Aunt Lizzie.

Bess, our eldest sister who was four years older than me, had recently gone into service in Bristol as general maid for two maiden ladies. Though this eased Mam's financial burden a little, life was poorer without Bess. Nature had been generous at her birth, for Bess was not only beautiful, she was very clever indeed, the top scholar at school in English and Arithmetic — and the best pupil in painting, sewing and cookery. She was a mine of ingenious ideas to amuse the younger ones. It was sad that her gifts were being smothered by a life of tedious domestic chores which she hated.

However, she could be manipulative for her own ends. When she was older and working for a Jewish family in London, they thought they had a great bargain when Bess suggested that she paint fairies and gnomes on their little girl's white bedroom furniture. It was a great success, but Bess felt she had the best bargain for her mistress did the housework while she enjoyed using her artistic talent.

My brother Charlie was three years younger and very special. My parents had already suffered broken hearts with the loss of two toddler sons before he was born. But Charlie had a weak chest and had had two periods in a sanatorium. Gwen came next, an angelically fair girl win an angelically good nature. Last was Marie, an appealingly attractive sprite as dark as Gwen was fair, and very special too because she was the youngest.

We were a very mixed bunch with a variety of faults and virtues, and were fortunate to have the most selfless parents who would go hungry to ensure their family could eat. At that time the couple of shillings a week that Dad could have legitimately charged Granny for her board and lodging would have been a great help, for work in the Forest mines was grinding to a halt. Instead, Dad walked to Wales and got a job in the "Six Bells" colliery near Abertillery. This time he lodged with Mam's oldest sister Polly, who had married a man much older than herself and was childless. She only took a pittance off Dad for his keep, but even so he could not afford to come home when Mam gave birth to me.

When he answered the letter telling him of my arrival, he wrote back adding kisses for "My little fat Polly". This nickname stuck although I was christened Winifred after one of Dad's seven step-sisters who was very kind to us.

Most of his step-sisters were a blessing, although they were a very mixed bunch. But Granny treated them all the same: "I don't believe in makin' poop o' one and puddin' of another!" she declared. Between Granny's sweet homely features and Grandad's handsome ones, they produced some beautiful girls. One of them, Beatie, was too alluring for her own good, but she managed to find a husband before the baby arrived. All seven had gone into service at the age of 14, becoming household treasures for their lucky mistresses. Olive, the eldest, married a young and ambitious miner, and when an uncle left him two cottages, he sold them and took Olive and their baby to America, to the mining area of Illinois. They had two daughters, both of whom went to college and married professional men. They were clever and good-looking, and nice people into the bargain.

Gladys came next. She was a bit dour and serious like Grandad, and married late. But she turned into a proper softie when she had a baby boy. Besotted with him, she was overjoyed when he won first prize at a baby show at around a year old. But fate was unbearably cruel for by the time he was 18 months old, he was dead of cancer of the kidneys. Her marriage didn't survive the blow, and she turned to religion and spiritualist meetings to try and find some solace for her grief. She made a second and happy marriage many years later, but gave up her home to live with and take care of Granny and Grandad until they died.

Winnie followed Gladys, a gentle placid character who worked her way up from scullery maid to cook in her first place in Bristol. She then moved to London, at one time being cook to one of the Gaiety Girls, I think Lily Elsie was the name. Winnie fell in love with London, its pageantry and infinite variety. She spent her half-days off walking through its famous highways and byways. This meant that she could be a great help to Granny by sending her most of her wages. Winnie felt herself rich just to be breathing London's foggy air.

After Winnie came Beatie who had so badly blotted her copybook, and after her came Elsie.

Not only Granny, but everyone was entranced and puzzled as to how such a flower of a creature had taken root in our humble village. A fragile-looking beautiful child, innately fastidious, sweet-natured and unassuming. Granny couldn't help making pudding of this one, as indeed did all around her. It was no surprise that by the time she was 19 Elsie had achieved promotion from second housemaid to lady's maid. Her mistress took her everywhere — abroad as well as to grand houses, where Elsie probably looked the most aristocratic of all there.

However sadly some of Elsie's fragile refinement was due to the tuberculosis that was lying dormant, only showing in her tendency to be "chesty". One day she fainted when doing her mistress's hair. A doctor was called in at once, and he diagnosed the problem. At the mention of the word "tuberculosis", Elsie's value in her mistress's eyes melted away and she was sent home immediately with a month's wages.

Granny used every source at her disposal and, forgetting her pride, anything she could beg from anyone in her efforts to save this treasured child. The odds were too great. Bowed in body and spirit, Granny lost the battle. She often said that had it not been for the help she received from Great-Aunt Lizzie she would not have had the will to go on living when Elsie died.

My favourite aunt was Lois. I loved it when she came home to Granny on her holidays. She powdered my nose with scenty pages from a tiny booklet, dabbed some of her precious perfume behind my ears, and tried to turn me into a ballet dancer. Her mistress had given her a ticket to see the great ballerina Anna Pavlova dancing "The Dying Swan". Lois couldn't get over it — it made her cry to talk about it. As it was too late for her to become a ballet dancer, she thought I might be one instead. She took my boots off and spent her two weeks of holiday putting me through the exquisite torture of trying to walk on my toes. She had no luck.

Auntie Phyllis was the youngest. Pert and very pretty, and a natural comedienne. I have seen the grown-ups convulsed with laughter at her mimicry. She knew lots of saucy songs and recitations, and could dance the Charleston like a real chorus girl. No-one guessed then that the same fate lay in wait for Elsie was also lying in wait for Phyllis. She was the last of the seven to be married, and settled down in the Cotswolds not far from where Lois lived. Lois had two children, a girl and a boy, and at that time her husband was away in the war. Phyllis's husband was working away from home as well. They also had two children, but when Phyllis's second child was a few months' old, Lois found Phyllis in a coma lying by the copper in the washhouse.

Phyllis was admitted to a nearby sanatorium, and she never gave up hope that she would get better and come home, even when the plague had reduced her to a living skeleton too weak to lift the shawl round her shoulders. Right to the end she would tell jokes to try and cheer up her visitors. After her death, Lois took in her children and brought them up as her own. They all enriched our childhood with pennies from their meagre wages, discarded clothing from their jobs, and their company.

CHAPTER
TWO

Tell Me, Auntie!

One Sunday, when the weather was gloriously sunny, Dad had walked a couple of miles to help my Grandad put a new roof on his pigsty, my eldest sister was in Bristol in domestic service and Mam had taken my two younger sisters and brother through a woodland path to the main road with the hope they might have the thrill of seeing a car go by. It was a lovely spot, where we sat under the shade of nearby oaks on a grassy bank dotted with daisies. There Bess used to split the daisy stems with a fingernail and make me bracelets, rings and necklaces, assuring me that I looked like a fairy queen — I always believed her. Today, though, I had chosen to stay home with old Auntie.

As a treat, I used to be allowed to fetch out her huge family Bible with its brass clasp and lurid coloured illustrations, in which she had pressed oak, beech and chestnut leaves that she had brought home all the way from California.

They were at least three times the size of British leaves.

Not only did I love old Auntie for her dear self, but also because she had actually been to America where Mary Pickford, my icon of the golden curls and the world's cinematic sweetheart, lived. Crippled with arthritis, wrinkled and frail, Auntie's memories made her magic to me.

Now we had the cottage to ourselves and I asked "Can I fetch the Bible to 'ave a look at the pictures, Auntie, please?"

"Yes, my wench, but put the kettle over the fire and make me a cup of tea first."

I did as she bid me. Then lifted down the heavy book and set it on the table in front of her. The first page of the Bible was almost filled with the dates of the births and deaths of our forebears. I worked out that she was nearly 84 years old.

"Be you really 84 next week, Auntie?"

"Yes, my little wench, and I was born upstairs in this very cottage, but I was only nine years old when I 'ad to go out in the world to earn my livin' and I can remember that day as though it were yesterday, though clang me if I can remember where I put me walkin' stick from one minute to the next."

To me, the idea of someone three years younger than me going to work was fantastic. It made little sense, and I asked "Why did you 'ave to leave 'ome when you was only nine years old, Auntie?"

"Well, 'twas like this, my wench. Up till then you couldn't 'ave found an 'appier little wench than me. My uncle, your great-great-uncle, owned a quarry and my dad worked for 'im. 'Twas only small but all the other men in the village was miners and far worse off than us. My mam was a wonderful woman, not a mean streak in her, a splendid manager who kept us well fed, well clothed, and helped out our neighbours when she could. Dad worshipped 'er. I often saw him giving her a kiss when he thought nobody was lookin'.

"He loved her too much perhaps, for by the time I was nine years old I had two little sisters and there was another baby on the way. Everyone hoped it would be a boy this time. As before, mother was having Mrs. Phillips for the birth. Though not officially trained as a nurse, all the women revered her for the helpful and wonderful way she understood their suffering and minimised it by her caring attitude. She had a grown-up family herself and understood. This time, though, all didn't go well for Mam,

Mrs. Phillips sent someone to fetch Dad home and run two miles to get the doctor, for the nearest hospital was 20 miles away.

"But the doctor had already gone to another patient in his horse and trap, so by the time he got here it was too late. He saved the baby, a boy, but poor Mother died. Even now I can't bear to remember how cruel this blow was for my Dad. If he hadn't had we children I'm sure he would have thrown himself into the grave with her. He paid too dearly for his little son. Now he had the problem of four children and the necessity to go back to work to keep them.

"I was old for my years and sharp with it, but even with all the help our over-burdened neighbours could give us, it was beyond my capabilities to run the home. Fate then paid a cruel trick on my Dad. A few days previously, a woman had come from the Yorkshire coal mining area for a holiday with some relatives at the top of the village. She was grossly fat, nearly blind and oozing with hypocrisy. Perhaps desperation clouded Father's judgement, for when she offered to move in and housekeep for him he felt he had no option but to agree. I could see through her from the start and hated her. Father moved downstairs so that she could have the double bed upstairs.

"Out of their love for Mother, our neighbours did most of the caring for the baby, who Dad named Enoch. My judgement of this woman, whose name was Sarah, soon proved only too right. She was a greedy sadistic tyrant who obviously hated children. Children can be harsh judges and I made no allowances that her mean spirit might be feeding on her own miseries — being nearly blind and cruelly over-weight, and not really wanted by anyone for herself. I only know she starved us to put the bulk of the food down her own huge belly. She scarcely ate anything when father was about and made sure there was always enough food for him. She hardly moved from the chair by the fireplace, while making sure I did all the heavy chores about the house. She did not even make the effort to waddle down to the bucket privy at the bottom of the garden. She used a bucket in the little indoor washhouse and made me empty it.

"But it was seeing my little sister go hungry that made me the angriest. As I was making up the fire one day, I told her I would tell father she was starving us. She grabbed hold of my long hair and pulled it with such viciousness that some came out by the roots and my head was left bleeding.

"I told her how I hated her and I'd beg Father to get rid of her. 'He will,' I cried, 'when he sees what you've done to my hair.' 'And I'll tell him different!' she sneered, 'I'll tell him you stumbled over the fender and I saved you from fallin' into the fire by grabbin' your hair. I'll tell him too what a nasty little hussy you are, cheeky, and won't take notice of what I say.' The thought that she could turn my Father against me was unbearable. 'I hate you, you're wicked and God will punish you!' I shouted at her. It made her that mad, she picked up the poker and threw it at me. Luckily it missed.

"When Father gave me a gentle scolding that evening, I knew I'd lost the battle. It seemed like a blessing from heaven when a neighbour told us that her daughter was leaving her job in service to get married and there was a vacancy for a scullery-maid in the house, and that she would ask for it for me. Dad and me jumped at the chance so I wrote and was offered the job. Until Mam died, Dad always spared the twopence a week for me to go to the Dame school in the village to learn the three Rs, so I could do sums, read well and write a proper letter. The Dame said I was the brightest child she had ever taught, but in them days there was no rules

16

about your age for workin', and we were in sore need.

"It meant almost a 40-mile walk to get there. Poor Dad, he had mortgaged himself to give Mam a far finer funeral than he could afford and he couldn't pay for me to go by cart. So, almost before dawn broke one summer Saturday morning before my 10th birthday, Father and me started out. He carried my clothes in two bundles on a stout stick across his shoulders. To cut the distance, Father decided to go as the crow flies rather than use the main roads for most of the distance. He carried some bread and cheese and a bottle of cold tea as refreshment for us.

"After the first couple of miles the countryside changed from woodlands to farmland and orchards. There were very few dwellings, but when we did a short distance on the main road, we refilled our bottle with water from a horse trough and quenched our thirst, for the weather was turning warm. Father tried to make the trek interesting, pointing out the badger holes, and the different birds, and spotting the wild sorrel for us to chew. But 11 miles from home I felt terrible hungry and my blistered feet were bleeding and my legs were weak from tiredness.

"When we came to a little stream, Father bade me sit down and take my boots and stockings off. He filled our bottle from the stream to bathe my feet, then wrapped them in some dock leaves before I put on my stockings. I couldn't bear the pressure of the boots so he hung them on his shoulder stick.

"Hardly able to hold back my tears, I trudged on. It was getting on towards the evening when Father stopped at a shabby little farmhouse. A woman about 60 years old, as shabby and run down as the farmhouse itself, was feeding some fowls. Dad approached her and asked if we could beg a night's shelter in her barn and explained where we were going. Her pinny was torn and dirty, her face lined and careworn, but her eyes lit up into pools of kindness.

"Not only could we have shelter of the barn, she brought us out two feather pillows, filled our bottle with milk and gave both of us a huge hunk of home-made bread, each topped with a thick slice of her home-cured fat bacon. In front of my eyes she seemed to turn into an angel. 'You go and lie down, my wench,' Dad advised me kindly. It was still light, and Dad picked up the saw lying by a pile of tree limbs and sawed logs for her till it was dark. I slept like one of them logs and never noticed the mice running over me.

"Next morning, when he took our pillows back and thanked her, she gave us some bread and cheese each. 'All the angels bent in 'eaven.' Dad remarked as we plodded on."

CHAPTER
THREE

Life in Service

"At last we arrived. Huge wrought iron gates with a lodge each side fronted an imposing drive flanked with hydrangeas which led up to the grand residence I was going to work in. I put my boots back on and hobbled to the servants' entrance with Father. A kitchen maid answered the door and took us along a great stone corridor and into the kitchen.

"That kitchen was so big, my wench, you could 'ave put this cottage into it and still have room to spare. I could see the scullery through a doorway. The cook seemed very nice. She shook hands with Father and ordered the maid who had let us in to make some tea and refreshment for him and to take me to the attic room I was to share with her and the first kitchen maid. The maid told me her name was Annie.

" 'You be lucky the cook's in a good humour today, she's all right really but when her gout and her stomach trouble do play her up, 'tis look out.' She had carried one bundle of my clothes and me the other. 'Another good thing about this job,' Annie said, 'they give you your uniform.' "

"As scullery maid, like the kitchen maid, I wouldn't have to change into afternoon uniform. But the uniform laid out for me on the bed was much too large an' I looked a right comic when I went back to the kitchen. Father was ready to go. I went with him to the door. His eyes were filled with tears. 'I'll be a good girl,' I told him. He couldn't speak, just gave me a big hug and kiss and walked away.

"The sight of him with the empty stick on his shoulder is as plain to me now, my wench, as the day it 'appened. I can't begin to tell you how strange and homesick I felt when Dad was out of sight. Everything was so big and different. The upstairs had eaten their luncheon, and the china, glass and silver used in the dining room was washed up by the head housemaid and parlour maid in the butler's pantry, but there were plenty of pots and pans for me to do.

"One kitchen maid was laying up the table in the servants' hall whilst the other carried in the food. The servants' hall was across the passage from the kitchen. I thought it was enormous and quite grand, although the curtains, rug and chairs were shabby faded remnants from the

21

upper regions. A huge table and chairs occupied most of the room and were already sat on by what seemed a crowd of servants. The butler and lady's maid ate in their own little sitting room. The cook could have had the same privilege but she preferred to sit at the head of the servants' table for her dinner and supper meals. There were two lads and an old man among the eight female indoor staff, and they all seemed to be staring at me.

" 'This is Lizzie, our new scullery maid,' the cook said.

" 'er's a bit of a midget, be 'er from the orphanage?' the old man asked her.

"The cook told him I'd been recommended by the girl who had left to get married. I was a bit young, nine years old, and not to be teased. Them kind words of that cook made me love her and determined to do my best. The next good thing was the food, plenty of meat, vegetables and gravy, with rice pudding or treacle tart to follow.

"I was astonished that the servants could take such food for granted. I was hungry but my appetite was spoilt thinking how I wished I could have sent some of it home. All the years I was in the job, it was torture to me to see good leftovers put in the waste bin."

"Was it a hard job, Auntie?"

"These days you'ld think it was. My job was mainly washing the pots and pans and scrubbing the downstairs passages and the kitchen floor. I was too short to reach the big sink and had to stand on a box. One day when I was trying hard to scrub the burnt bits off a saucepan, I toppled over into the sink. It made the cook double up with laughter. So did all the other servants when they 'eard. I even laughed myself.

"Although the food there was very good, I used to eat the scrapings from the saucepan, crying sometimes because I couldn't do some magic and send it home. It was a long time before I could reach the sink without a box.

"Though her temper scared me at times, the cook was very good to me. She gave me the sharp end of her tongue when her gout and indigestion got on her nerves, but she was like a mother hen to me. She was a very good-living woman and guided me into womanhood as me mother would have wished. It wasn't hard for her, for I only had one idea in my mind, and that was to save up every penny I could and grow to sixteen years old, when I intended to go back and be Father's housekeeper and look after my sisters and brother.

"To this end I collected anything that was thrown away that the other servants didn't lay claim to. I would accept their cast-off clothing rather than buy new for myself. They called me Lizzie Scrat, but it was in good humour. They felt for me losing my mother.

"Despite the shadow of homesickness, my spirits were buoyed up by the constant daydream of going back home, grown-up and with my savings, and to throw out that Sarah and look after them all. I hoped that when my sister Tryphena was 10 years old, she could have a job with me. As servants left or got promoted, there were frequent vacancies for the humbler jobs.

"How cruelly this dream was shattered. I was coming twelve years old when I got the letter written for Dad by the chapel minister saying Tryphena had died suddenly from brain fever, 'tis what they call meningitis today. Father begged me not to grieve too much, Tryphena was in a better place in heaven with Mother. I tried to find comfort in his words but I couldn't visualise this place called heaven nor see Tryphena as a spirit. I wanted her back home, a little girl of flesh and blood that I could hug and kiss and look after. The terrible feeling of loss went slowly.

"I almost left my job to go home, but cook said I should do more good to help by earning my keep and waiting until I was older. I could have had a week's paid holiday every year but I chose to have that extra week's money and stay on. I could not 'ave shared my home with that Sarah, who was still there."

CHAPTER
FOUR

Friends and Companions

"Two of the housemaids were sisters. They came from Suffolk, and two nicer girls it would be a job to meet. Their names were Muriel and Dora, and both had beautiful grey eyes, trim figures, and an abundance of dark brown hair. Dora at 21 was by two years the younger. Nature must have been in a very benevolent mood when she fashioned Dora for she had a neat pert nose, rosebud mouth, lovely complexion and a natural curl in her hair, all finished off with nice even white teeth.

"With Muriel, Nature must have been in a more slap-dash mood, for her nose was a broad snub, her lips were too full and undefined, her complexion muddy, her hair straight, and she had two slightly protruding teeth. But her character was as sunny and cheerful as was her sister's.

"Not surprisingly, Dora had a steady young man back home. He and Dora could read and write, and his letters (the latest of which she always carried about in her apron pocket for surreptitious reading) kept their courtship flourishing for they only saw each other on her annual holiday. It was a few weeks after coming back after visiting home that we noticed Dora frequently looked as though she had been crying. Muriel seemed subdued as well. Then after several months Dora, who seemed to me to be getting fat, left to go home and get married.

"The second kitchen maid asked for and was given Dora's position, and I was made up to second kitchen maid. The new scullery-maid was called Ruth and was a big plain girl from an orphanage. She was a bit slow, but a good worker. I liked Ruth and felt very sorry for her when she told me what life had been like in the orphanage.

"She had been named Ruth Brown because she had been found wrapped up in a brown shawl on the orphanage doorstep by a servant called Ruth. She amazed me because she didn't seem to be curious or to worry about where she came from. Her great love was for a wooden doll with an arm missing that someone had given her. She took it to bed with her and, when she thought no-one was about, she talked to it, kissed it, and pretended to spoon-feed it as though it were a real baby.

"I never said anything because I ached to see my own little brother and sister, so understood some of what she felt.

"Then when I was twelve, the head kitchen maid got married, to one of the estate workers, a cow man I believe. She came in daily for a while, then left to have a baby and I was made First Kitchen Maid. By now I thought the world of Cook. She treated me almost like I was her daughter so I never asked for an upstairs job.

"The new second kitchen maid seemed quite old to us young girls as she was in her early thirties. A gentle good-looking woman called Jeannie, her looks were marred by a large purple birthmark on her cheek. It so embarrassed her that it almost seemed she was apologizing to the world for it. But being an extraordinarily nice person, she didn't seem to resent me being so much younger than her and yet over her in the kitchen.

"The more I came to know her, the more I thought what a pity it was that she wasn't married to some nice man who deserved her. Then out of the blue the notion struck me that there was someone we knew who would just fit the bill.

"Mr. James was a widower about 50 who came every couple of weeks to wind all the clocks in the house and keep them in good order. He was a sad man whose wife had died some years previously, which he seemed unable to get over, but he was a gentle kind man with a club foot who, despite a built-up shoe, limped a bit. He used to say 'Hello, little missy' to me and very much appreciated his cup of tea and piece of cake in the kitchen, and a chat with Cook, who held him in high regard.

"The more I thought about it, the more I wished he and Jeannie would take to each other and get married, but she was so shy in his presence it seemed hopeless. Then one day, as Cook and us kitchen maids were having a cup of tea before starting on that evening's dinner, Ruth told us about one of the orphanage staff who could tell fortunes by reading tea leaves in tea cups. Apparently, after drinking the tea, Ruth said you had to turn the cup round three times, then put it upside down on the saucer and tap that bottom of the cup three times. From the pattern made by the tea-leaves, the drinker's fortune could be told. Of course I knew nothing about fortune-telling, but when it came to my turn to read the others' cups (Cook wouldn't take part), I simply told them things from what I had heard them saying about their lives, adding bits that I felt sure applied to almost everyone.

"They were all so impressed that it gave me an idea for the next time we read the tea-leaves. This time, when I read Jeannie's cup I put on an air of deep concentration. 'I can see a man here, Jeannie. He's thinking of you a lot but you don't seem to notice him.' Jeannie blushed and shook her head. I went on, 'There's something unbalanced about him. He's got something wrong that upsets his balance a bit. Look,' I showed them, 'See how some tea-leaves come down in two lines from the main one, and one side line is shorter than the other, so it may be he's a cripple.'

" 'Eeh,' burst out Ruth, 'That sounds like Mr. James!'

" 'And look,' I said, my imagination going full pelt, 'There's sadness as well. See these two tea-leaves falling, that means tears. Jeannie, I reckon you should give him a smile when he comes to the kitchen, not hide away like you usually do!'

"Emboldened by a longing to see these two lonely people find contentment and company from each other, I hoped I wasn't doing wrong. I felt sure Mr. James was too nice a man to be put off by Jeannie's birthmark, and do you know, my wench, it worked! When I finally left the household, they were planning to get married, and the lovely Jeannie was transformed with happiness."

CHAPTER
FIVE

Grief Has No Barriers

"Every Autumn the master and mistress went to Scotland for grouse-shooting for a month. They always took some of the indoor staff and left the rest of us to clean the great manor thoroughly from top to bottom. During the four weeks they were away, the elderly butler left in charge of us allowed some laxity in our lives.

"When the cook realized it was my 15th birthday, she gave me three pairs of hand-knitted stockings, collected just over the sum of a guinea from the other servants, made a huge iced cake for us all, and I had my first birthday card. I thought it was the most beautiful picture. It was big, signed by them all and covered with coloured roses and golden lettering. I still 'ave it in the box with me will. What a wonderful feeling it was to think other people were so kind to me. I was happier than I thought possible since Tryphena had died. I put the guinea with me savings in my little locked cash-box. No Scrooge gloated more over money than I did.

"Soon, soon I would be able to give my notice in and go home.

"It was a great shock when the butler summonsed us all to the servants' hall. He had bad news. The family were returning home right away. The mistress's mother had died suddenly. She was quite old, but her death from a heart attack was a shock. All the upper servants who had met her always spoke highly of her. She was in their opinion a 'real lady', undemanding and gentle. The mistress almost worshipped her and was in a dreadful state, with the doctor attending her.

"Ah, my wench, death hits us all. Kings and Queens are as powerless to escape it as them that clean their boots and sweep their chimneys. Because they were so above us in their living, and had so many of the blessings that money brings, the servants didn't feel great pity, but none laughed or joked or smiled, out of respect. All the normal hustle came to a stop. It was as though the very manor itself was in mourning.

"Then my own unbearable grief came in a black-edged letter. At first my mind could not accept what was written in it. Again it was from the chapel minister. A terrible form of influenza had hit the village. The minister himself had lost a 13-year-old daughter and it had taken my father and little sister, to join my mother in heaven as he put it.

"This double blow was too much for my mind. I lost my reason, I couldn't stop screaming, I hated the Almighty himself. I couldn't eat or drink or keep still. My lady's doctor was called in to see me. I was given sedatives and a talking-to by Cook, and then by the doctor himself. It was he who made me realize I still had a little brother who would need my love, and that I must make sure that he was provided for. But I could not carry out my duties, just kept crying non-stop tears. Cook, God bless her, eventually gave in my notice for me and I was actually summonsed into the presence of my mistress.

"In the six years I had worked there, I had never spoken to her. I had seen her through the window sometimes, a regal beautiful figure of a woman getting into the carriage to go visiting, and at Christmas when a dance was put on for the staff. The family would attend the beginning and wish us all a Happy New Year.

"The butler escorted me to the little sitting room adjoining her bedroom. He knocked on the door, ushered me in and went away. I could hardly recognise the sad figure sitting dressed in black. She seemed to have shrunk. Her face, hair and eyes all seemed to have a patina of greyness. Her eyes were dull and sunken from the swelling brought on by weeping. The sight of her and the feeling I had that her heart too was broken with her grief brought the tears to my own face. It was difficult for her to find composure to speak.

" 'I'm sorry,' she said, 'that you are leaving us due to the sad circumstances at your home.' At this, my composure went. I burst into tears and told her about my Dad and my two little sisters gone and that I must go home to look after my little brother.

" 'And so you shall, my dear. I'll arrange for you to go home in the next couple of days. You shall be taken to the railway station with your luggage and this,' she said, handing me a pretty little box. 'It's the wages you are owed and something for the years of very good service Cook says you have given us.'

"Oh, my wench, I did feel sorry for that poor lady. I could tell, like me, her heart was broken and in a way it put us on the same level. I wanted to hug her and I could see by the expression in her eyes that she felt the same towards me, but it would never have done.

"All I could do was say, 'Thank you, ma'am,' and my goodness, I had something to thank her for. As well as the bit of wages due to me, she had put 10 guineas in the little box. I felt like a rich woman. Now I could look after my little brother and throw that wicked Sarah out. How I blessed that lady.

"Only two days later, all my saved bits and pieces and my clothes were packed up and loaded in a trap and I was saying good-bye to the cook, who I had grown to love, and to the servants. Many of them had become my friends. The cook had parcelled me enough food to live on for a week.

"I felt all mixed-up. In six years my life there had become my reality, and thoughts and plans of home the dream that fed my future hopes. Now that dream had been reduced to crumbs, but the thought of seeing and caring for my little brother began to overwhelm me.

"When the young groom had unloaded my bags and boxes and put them on the train, his face flushed up and then went pale as he said to me, 'I be sorry you be leavin', Lizzie, you 'ave never took any notice o' me but I kept wishin' you would. I would 'ave like you to 'ave been my sweetheart.' Then he put his arm round me, kissed my cheek and hurried away.

"I was too took aback to answer him, but a lovely warm feeling went through me. That some man had thought of me as a sweetheart! A little sweetness stirred in the bitter dregs of my thoughts. I realised I was a woman. I was 15 years old."

CHAPTER
SIX

Going Home and Making a Living

"As the train gathered speed, I could hardly contain my excitement.

"I was really going home, going to see the little brother who was a stranger to me, someone to love, someone to care and work for. It suddenly seemed too good to be true. Perhaps the train would have an accident, or my heart would stop from beating too fast, but at last we stopped at the little station halt about 2 miles from the cottage.

"As a child I had known the man in charge but I was surprised when, after studying me quizzically for a few minutes, he said, 'Well, clang me, it's Lizzie Mason after all these years. I be glad to see you for the sake of that little brother of yours. Me and the missis do feel for you, my wench, losing your dad and little sister so sudden. Your uncle saw to it they had a tidy funeral, though. Your dad had been poorly for a long time. I be afeared this Sarah done a poor job o' lookin' after them since your poor Mother went. My word, you look as though you've brought your job back home with you.'

"I told him how things in this grand house I worked in was put out for rubbish but I'd collected it. Now I would have to get it delivered to the house. 'Don't thee worry about that, my wench. Old Annie Trump 'ave still got her donkey and cart, and 'er'll be glad to earn a sixpence fetching this stuff for thee. I'll call in on 'er on me way 'ome from work. Thee'll 'ave it afore the morning's out.'

"I picked up all I could manage to carry, including Cook's basket of food and, after thanking him, started home. Oh my wench, I soon realised what 'ome and the lovely forest and the people of my childhood meant to me. I was crying with a mixture of misery and happiness. Every daisy and blade of grass on the verges seemed precious and I could have hugged the beautiful great oak tress.

"As the cottage come into sight, I was amazed to see that Father had been building a small extension on it and that it was nearly finished. Yet an air of neglect was lying over everything. The gate was falling off its hinges, the garden had gone to weeds, only a stray flower was open here and there on the path borders. I thought I would pick these on the morrow and take them to put on the graves. Poor Father, I found out later that he had been ailing for a long time and was too weak to fight the influenza.

"My own legs seemed to turn to jelly as I approached the door. The cosy little living room that Mother had kept so clean, with shiny black-leaded grate, shining brass rod under the mantelpiece and polished fire irons and fender, rag rugs which were shaken every day after she had scrubbed the stone-flagged floor, the table and chairs and ornaments on the mantelpiece dusted, was now a squalid unkempt slum.

"I hardly noticed the obesely fat Sarah sat by the fireside for my eyes were drawn only to the sad-eyed little boy who was putting some wood on the fire. I went down on my knees and took him in my arms, a shabby, dirty little bag of bones and, oh, I can't tell you, my wench, how precious that little brother was to me.

"I was crying and hugging him, saying 'It's me, it's your big sister Lizzie come home from service to look after you. Wash your hands and sit at the table, I've got something nice for you to eat.'

"Poor little fellow, he looked so bewildered. I followed him into the back kitchen where a bowl contained some dirty soapy water. I threw it on the garden and found some clean in the bottom of a bucket. I couldn't find a clean plate, so laid him a feast out on the wrapping Cook had put the various bits of food in. 'Go on, Enoch,' I told him, 'eat up till your belly can't hold any more.'

"I kept on hugging and kissing him between mouthfuls. Poor little boy, he was so bewildered, but he looked up at me with his big sad eyes all friendly and I worshipped him. All the love I had saved for my family was concentrated and finding an outlet on him.

"You might think me 'ard, my wench, but all the love I felt for my little brother was equalled in the hate I felt for that Sarah. The sight of the food I put in front of Enoch made her drool. She began to whine for some, telling me that after he had paid for the funerals, Father's brother gave her one guinea and she had not seen him since.

"I could not bear to even look at the gross figure oozing over the side of the wooden armchair, chin on chin coated with residues of food. She must be got out of the house before I could sleep in it. I knew it meant parting with some of my precious savings but I had a plan.

With the temptation of three golden guineas in my hand, a lot of money in them days, I went up to her relatives and offered them the money in return for taking Sarah and her belongings out of my house. I suggested they used some of it to send her back to Yorkshire.

"They justifiably stood out for another guinea and then they came with me to heave her out of the chair and take her out of my life.

"Invigorated by seeing the back of her, Enoch and me made enough trips to the village well to fetch water to fill the big copper in the washhouse. I planned to get up at dawn the next morning and light a fire under it, for my great desire was for buckets and buckets of hot soapy water with which to scrub my cottage clean from corner to corner.

"In bed that night, I thought of all the things I could make with the bits and pieces I had brought home with me — curtains for the windows, cushion covers, rag mats, all making my home comfy and cheerful. Wallowing in anticipation, I felt sorry for rich women who had everything done for them.

"D'you know, my wench, life is best when you're needed and must make efforts. Now I could put all my efforts to looking after Enoch and getting a living without going into service and leaving him. I made my plans. I had got some money, enough to employ a builder to put the cottage to rights if I did the labouring. With Father's extension finished I should have two good-sized bedrooms and one small one.

"I would take in lodgers. I could have the little back bedroom, and two single beds in each of the others could cater for Enoch and three lodgers.

"I struck a good bargain with the builder. He thought with a slip of a wench for a labourer he would have an easy time, but he recounted countless times that it was the hardest work he had ever done, keeping up with me. My hands had been toughened by years of washing-up but they were bleeding and calloused by the end of the first week, before they toughened up to the demands I put on them. By bedtime every bone in my body ached, but I was happy as a lark as my little house was put into good shape.

"I put to good use all the throw-outs I had saved from my job. I made the curtains, cushion covers and pillow-cases, pegged rag-rugs and all manner of like things. I don't think the villagers took to me much. I had no time to gossip, no time for any man's intentions, and was altogether too dour for a girl not yet 16 years old. Even the biggest scandalmongers among them had nothing to conjecture about when I took in three male lodgers.

"I think they pitied me, but oh my wench, I can't tell you the joy I felt getting plenty of good food down Enoch and keeping him clean and tidy. He was such a lovely little boy and helped me anyway he could. My only worry with him was his nasty little cough which continued despite the tonics I got for him.

"I was lucky with my lodgers. The builder's brother, a man about 50 years old, was the first. He was a widower living with his married son and sensitive enough to realise the daughter-in-law wasn't happy about it. He was a carpenter in steady work. The other two were a pair of Welsh cousins, miners, who had fell in love with the Forest and got work here in the pit nearest to this village.

"I made my conditions plain before I took them in. No drunkenness or bad language, though I didn't object if they went to the village pub for the company of their mates. Lodging money must be paid regularly, and it was none of my business if they went to Chapel or not. In return I would give them a clean home, good wholesome food and do their washing.

"How thankful I felt to that cook for the cooking and housewifery skills she had taught me. I don't know if it's true that the way to a man's heart is through his stomach but by creating a comfortable domestic life and good food I earned their respect and consideration. I never had to put a spade in the garden, or empty the bucket privy, sweep the chimney or pay for little household repairs. They cleaned out the pigsty and chicken shed, and grew the vegetables, and I cooked the results to heap on their plates.

"It brought me a good living and a chance to put a bit of money by. They were good lodgers and they were good years. The men hardly ever ailed with more than a bad cold. Then I would dose them with plenty of my herbal tea and cosset them for a couple of days. Enoch seemed to go down every winter with a chesty cough no matter what I did, but he grew into a fine looking fellow and was as good as gold to me. I did my best to keep him out of the pit, but because there were no other jobs at the time he wouldn't be persuaded."

CHAPTER
SEVEN

Love Comes to
Aunt Lizzie

"By the time he was 21, Enoch was courting a nice pretty girl of nineteen from another village. Their courting was mostly by letter. She couldn't read or write but I had paid for Enoch to go to the Dame's school, as my Dad had paid for me to go, so he could read, write and cipher. Someone had to read her letters to her in her job and they got her a lot of teasing and envy from the other maids.

"Enoch turned into a bigger scrat than I had been. As well as working in the pit he took on every odd job that came his way. And, under the ancient right of the Forest of Dean, he kept a flock of sheep to graze freely. He couldn't bear the waiting to get married.

"About that time the father of my two Welsh lodgers died and they decided to go back to Wales for the sake of their broken-hearted mother. I had to keep the money coming in, so I took in another lodger."

"Was he a good lodger as well, Auntie?"

"Oh my wench, he was one of the best men that ever lived. That was your great uncle John Webb. That's him in that big photo over me bed. He had never been married though he was 48 years old and, as you can see in that photo, a very handsome man."

"Why wasn't he married, then?"

"Well, you see, his ma went blind when she was quite a young woman and John was only a year old. His dad couldn't stand the misery of it. Instead of stopping to look after her he went to sea and after a bit he stopped writing, and she never knew what happened to him. He never came back. She had to go home with the baby and live with her widowed mother. John was grown-up and working the pit when his gran died and after that he just looked after his mam.

"When she died he couldn't stand living in the house without her so he let all his stuff go, gave it away mostly and took up lodgings with me. By the time he had been in my home for an hour I knew I loved him. He was one of nature's gentlemen, he had no evil in him. I didn't make no secret about how I felt for him, but he was very shy and had no great opinion of himself. It

47

was over four years before he proposed. It didn't take me half a minute to say yes.

"Oh my wench, I can't tell you how happy I was! Before John I'ld never gave any thought to my appearance, so long as I was clean and tidy I didn't bother, but when a man tells a woman she's beautiful, she becomes beautiful. That was how it was with John and me. I can tell you, my wench, when a man do love you for your spirit as well as your body, you be as near to heaven as you can get on this earth.

"Once I said yes, John was wantin' to get married right away. Enoch was feeling just the same about his sweetheart. Her name was Lizzie too. We decided to have a quiet double wedding but before that I gave half the cottage to Enoch. Him and John put in a dividing wall between us so they could have their privacy. I still had my first lodger, Ernie, but he was willin' to go into the little back bedroom. He was no trouble and fitted in as homely as another chair by the fireside.

"There was talk in the village, and it was quite right that we were a pair of skinflints, havin' such quiet sober weddings. It didn't worry us — we were contented as two pairs of turtle-doves.

"Every year, just as they do now, a grand fair was put on in the Speech House grounds in the middle of the forest. John was determined to show me off. He bought me a beautiful pale green silk crinoline dress, a Dolly Vardin hat with a pink rose in every dip in the wide brim and trimmed with pale green ribbon. Not satisfied with that, he bought me a pale green silk parasol to match and some extra curls to pin to my own on each side of my cheeks. We went all the way to Gloucester in a hired pony and trap to buy them.

"I hardly knew myself in all that finery. John walked me around the fairground as though I was the Queen of Sheba. After that day people called me Lady Webb behind my back. I didn't care. But what a sensation some silks and ribbon can cause!

"What I wanted more than anything was to have a child but it was not to be. The next best thing happened. Young Lizzie told us she was having a baby. She and I knitted and sewed and crocheted, and John and Enoch made the baby a lovely wooden cot, helped by Ernie who was now almost one of the family. Trouble was Enoch was nearly out of his mind with happiness. As well as working in the pit and seeing to his animals, he started to build an extension on their end of the cottage.

"He was coughing a lot, and young Lizzie and me scolded him and tried to steady him down, but he just laughed at us. Late in August, on a lovely warm day, Lizzie had her baby, a dear little boy they christened Charles Enoch. That was your dad, my wench, and that seven pound bundle of cuddle became the focus of our lives. Even Ernie would want to nurse and drool over him. As for Enoch, he seemed to grow a couple of inches taller with pride, but sideways he grew thinner, despite all the gruel and extra titbits we got down him.

"One bitterly cold wet November after his early shift at the pit, he went straight out into the forest to scrabble among the wet leaves for acorns to put by for winter feed for his pigs. It was fool's economy. When he staggered home with two buckets of acorns, he could hardly get his breath and had pains in the chest. Lizzie and I got him to bed and put a linseed meal poultice on his chest whilst John ran the two miles to get the doctor.

"Our efforts were in vain. Pleurisy turned into pneumonia and nothing the doctor or we could do could save him. 'Kep an eye on me little boy, Liz,' was the last word he gasped to me.

"Poor young Lizzie! Bewildered and grief-stricken, she understandably would not let me adopt the baby, for it was all she had. She let the cottage for 2/6d a week and went back to live with her mother, going out cleaning daily at the rectory and the pit owner's residence to keep them.

"Despite having the blessing of John, not for the first time life seemed to have lost its meaning for me. I could not bear the loss of this treasured brother and the cruel fate that had taken him so untimely. Melancholy, like an octopus, wrapped me in its tentacles. I lost the will and strength to get out of bed in the morning. The days which had never seemed long enough for all my busy plans stretched out like empty voids ending in sleepless nights.

"Poor John, he was wracked with misery caring for me. How deep his despair must have been for him to come up with the notion we should sail to California to seek our fortune in the gold fields over there.

" 'Just think, Lizzie,' he'ld say, 'we might be able to make a lot of money to bring back to England, enough to keep young Charlie out of the pit and maybe educate him to be a doctor or summat.'

"Such a thought was the strand I needed to clutch at to bring me back to some sort of sanity, and the enormity of the challenge acted like chloroform on my tortured mind. Of course, we had to tell Ernie about our plans, which would mean letting the cottage. It was Ernie who had the solution — he would rent it himself. He was sure his daughter-in-law would clean and do his washing for him. I was so pleased I let Ernie have the cottage rent free, providing he paid the rates and kept it in good order for our return."

CHAPTER
EIGHT

Off to America

"John did all the organising. The original Gold Rush was long over, when the migrants travelled across America by covered wagons, braving attacks by Indians to stake their claims or went on the long sea voyage from East to West coast. Now a railroad had been built from New York to California, and most of the area was taken over by big mining companies with different methods of extracting the gold. However, it was still a good place for a miner to earn good money.

"We were to sail from Southampton and I felt like a stranger was stepping out in my own shoes as we boarded the ship. Worse than the strangeness was the horror I felt when I saw the conditions we should be sailing under. I wondered how whosoever owned that ship could rest in his bed at night. My wench, 'tis cruel what men will do to their fellow creatures to profit out of them.

"To sail steerage, which was all we could afford, meant living in the bottom of the ship. All the men, about three hundred, slept one end, and all the women and children at the other. It was terrible crowded, a bunk about two feet wide for each person, with a bit of space above where our belongings had to fit in somehow. We each had a mattress and a pillow filled with straw but everything was dirty. The place stank where people and children had been sick and piddled. There was hardly any water to be had and sometimes it was so cold down there we had to go to bed without undressing.

"We were all given a spoon, knife and fork and plate which were rusty, and we had to look after them for the voyage. The food was terrible. We would have been quite satisfied with very plain fare, but our meals were made of poor quality stuff made much worse by the way it was cooked and served. We had to queue up for the steward to serve us, then find somewhere to sit and eat. There were hardly any tables or seats. The women with babies had these. We sat on our bunks, but the air was foul down there.

"The greatest blessing we had was being allowed to go on deck for some periods each day. If the weather permitted we ate up there. For some days John and I were too ill to eat. The nausea from sea-sickness was well-nigh unendurable, but somehow we always struggled up on deck. Dear John, he never grumbled at me nor I to him, for I knew he had taken this on for my sake. There is nothing like love to oil the wheels of endeavour. I even got a little comfort thinking poor dear Enoch would never have to suffer like it.

"Although we couldn't spend much time together, without John on board I think I would have thrown myself into the sea. The stewards were such low types of men, they couldn't behave themselves with the women. The poor women, they bit and fought them off as well as they could. I gave them, the stewards, such looks of hate they hardly ever tried to bother me.

"When first on board we were all seen by a doctor and passed as fit and healthy, and given cards to prove it, but by the time we landed we were all in poor shape. All the same, the relief of being back on land got our spirits soaring with hope.We stayed in a sort of boarding house for a night, a shabby, poor sort of place that served the immigrants, but it seemed a palace compared to the ship.

"A few of the passengers didn't survive the crossing. God knows how the early gold rush pioneers had found the courage to face the hardships of covered wagons, and hostile Indians to get to California. It took months for them, going slowly across the prairies and then the mountains. We were lucky for the railway had only been recently completed. Even then, it was a hard trip.

"I used to think of them women in the wagons as I looked out of the window on that long wearisome journey, and think how lucky I was not having to put up with all they had had to.

"When we got to the mining area it was terrible to see how huge areas of the lovely countryside had been ravished in the search for gold. To my mind, what they gained on the swings, they lost on the roundabouts as the saying goes. Living conditions were generally very rough. We thought ourselves lucky to get lodgings with a pair of Methodist missionaries, a man and his wife trying to put the fear of God into the miners, speaking out against the temptations of drink, gambling and bad women. They held outdoor sermons and indoor bible classes. To some they were a laughing stock but they never took offence.

"The lodgings were clean and fairly priced, but I knew we must start earning quickly ourselves, for our savings were running out. I needed also to have my time occupied to help battle with the strangeness of it all. Before long I had come up with an idea. It was my instincts that men always need feeding and that there were plenty of men here trying to feed themselves, and doing it poorly. I would set up a cookhouse.

"After searching and enquiries, I was able to rent a large rough wooden shed and managed to get some trestle tables, benches, a primitive cooking stove and enough pots and pans, cutlery and crockery to make a start. John helped me with all this before he looked for a job himself.

"There were some stores on the gold field, and travelling vendors would come with such things as dried apple and peaches and onions. I bought these cheap in quantity, as well as flour, lard and meat. I started making sweet and savoury pies, and my wooden shed soon filled with customers. Those that couldn't find room to sit bought my pies to eat outside.

"Before long, I was making enough for John and me to live on. But we had come aiming to earn much more and so John found a job, working for the prospectors that employed the tunnel system. It was gruelling work entailing the making of tunnels about 7 feet high and 5 feet wide, shoring them up with timber and removing the earth to be hydraulically washed for gold. John was now 52 years old, and he looked so tired it worried me. However, we soon began to put some savings by.

"After a couple of years, it was a nice amount and then came a stroke of luck. Our hosts decided to sell their boarding house and return to their native Illinois. John and I decided to borrow some money to add to our savings to buy it. We could then run it between us and I would carry on selling pies to the miners. All went well and although the gold was beginning to run out and the work was slowing down, with fewer new men coming, we prospered.

"Our plan was working out nicely. When we had paid for the boarding house, we began to have daydreams of returning to England, prosperous and seeing what we could do for our beloved young Charlie.

"John was a wonderful partner who helped greatly in the business. I marvelled often why I had been so lucky to have him for a husband. Real love can take you to heaven, my wench. But within a year or so I was wondering why the Almighty was being so cruel to me, for John became ill. He tried to hide it at first but he went off his food, his skin began to go yellow and he was growing weaker. Eventually I insisted on his seeing the doctor. He said that John had got a growth on the liver, and that there was no cure.

"I could not accept that John was dying. Desperation drives reason out of the window. I felt if I could bring him back home, back to the Forest and the people who knew and respected him, he would be saved, so I sold the boarding house to the first bidder and booked first class passages for the homeward journey.

"It took most of our savings."

CHAPTER
NINE

Life After John

"Whilst we were away young Lizzie had re-married to a handsome taciturn miner and returned to live in her cottage. She then proceeded to over-fill it with baby daughters. Though her husband demanded nothing except his weekly ounce of twist tobacco to chew, it was obvious they were having a great struggle to survive. Charlie got his share of affection from his mother but she was sadly lacking in the means to feed and dress her brood satisfactorily.

"With our savings now reduced and John so ill I could hardly help them at all. I was just starting to suffer from this drafted rheumatics that 'ave crippled me up so. It was unspeakably awful watching John get worse. In the end I was praying to the Almighty to take him.

"Now, don't cry, my wench, I knew that John would go to heaven and be in a much better place than we be in. Eh what's the time? I can't see the clock face properly."

"Five o'clock, Auntie."

"Well, my wench, you better put that Bible away and set the table ready for tea. Your mam will be back any minute. I think I'll just have a doze as I do feel so tired all the time."

As soon as she closed her eyes, her old head fell sideways and she was asleep, wrinkled, frail with misshapen knobbly fingers. It was hard to believe old Auntie had been through the times she had described. She had always been the figure in the armchair to which I had run to put my head in her lap when Mam was about to chastise me for my frequent misdemeanours. Her hand would cover the top of my head, and she would say "Leave 'er be, Maggie, you can't put old heads on young shoulders."

Mostly her lap was filled with the babies Mam produced, or with some patching or darning she struggled to finish despite her arthritic hands. She always left a bit of Nestles milk in the bottom of her tin for my little brother and me to scrape out.

Someone named Lloyd George had got her thanks almost as much as the Almighty. The precious 5 guineas she had hung on to for her funeral, to "put her under the ground tidy" without being a burden to her beloved Charlie, were in danger of being broken into when Lloyd

George brought in the 5 shillings weekly pension for the over-70s. Now it had gone up to 10 shillings a week and she sang the praises of Lloyd George and the Almighty for their munificence.

In return for living with her in her cottage, Dad worked in the garden and she accepted a share of vegetables, and when she had a stroke and lost the use of an arm and her face went lopsided and she dribbled, it was Dad that massaged her arm with goose grease every minute he was home and brought the use back in her arm and made her face straight again. Those two loved one another and I believe would have laid down their lives for each other.

Mam and the little ones came in, my brother very disappointed they had not seen a car go by. I was one up on them because before I was four years old I had actually had a ride in a car, all due to old Auntie. In the years before she had married John Webb, a young distant relative, a boy, had been left without means of support and would have had to go to the workhouse. Auntie had provided the means to feed and clothe him until he went to New Zealand, probably under some government scheme. Eventually he had become the manager of a rabbit-canning factory. We knew him as Uncle Alf.

With a well-paid job, he had saved enough to come to England to see his benefactor. For an out-of-this-world treat, he hired a car for the day to take Auntie, Mam, sister Bess, me and the baby to a place called Severn Beach. It was a tiny black car and was filled with petrol fumes, so by the time we had got to Severn Beach, I was ill with a dreadful headache and nausea. We were the only visitors to the spot.

Bess made the best of it, appreciating everything about the outing and gathering a nice lot of even-sized pebbles to play five stones with. For me, I can only remember the grey water, a grey ship, grey pebbles, and the black misery of feeling sick. At the time, shaking her head, Bess truthfully observed that I was a regular little misery guts. On the way home, Uncle Alf tried to distract me by teaching me a Maori war dance chant. I have no idea how to spell it but this is what it sounded like:

"COOMATI, COOMATI, COURA COURA
NA NA A PICK OI ME WOCKA TE TE TE RAH
OOPANI COOPANI TINGA TE TONGA TA
AKI AKI KIAKA
AKI AKI AH"

In my 88th year I can still remember it!

The pebbles were kept in Dad's shed at the bottom of the garden. I could never play five stones with them, the sight of them gave me a terrible nausea and headache.

Mam hadn't said anything about her leg paining her when she went for a walk so as not to disappoint Charlie, but when she got home it was badly swollen and very red and shiny. When Dad came home, he said it was a job for the doctor. Dad was a great believer in herbal medicine and never had the doctor for himself. Without even pulling a face, he would get down mugs full of his own bitter brews.

Thus the decision to call the doctor was not taken lightly — at the time it was the custom to pay the local doctor 5 shillings per family each quarter to be on his list. Even this modest sum was always in arrears, and a sixpence or shilling had to be got in order to persuade the doctor to come out. By dint of their own efforts, the people of the Forest of Dean, mostly miners, had made it possible to build a cottage hospital only about 3 miles from our village.

They named it the Dilke Hospital after their M.P., Sir Charles Dilke because, despite the marital scandal that marred his time in office, they were loyal to him for his efforts on the behalf of the miners.

On seeing her leg, the doctor ordered Mam there straightaway. As well as phlebitis, it was found that Mam suffered from a heart weakness. My 17-year-old sister Bess was sent for to come home from her job in domestic service in Bristol to look after us as the hospital said that Mam would be kept in for some weeks.

CHAPTER
TEN

Charlie's Story

One day when I got home from school, old Auntie was in bed in the tiny parlour downstairs she now slept in.

"'er be very tired today," Bess said.

Dad was gone to walk to the hospital to see Mam, so I sat with old Auntie as she ate her bit of supper.

"What 'appened after Great-Uncle John died?" I asked her.

"I just had to carry on, my wench, though the heart had gone out of me. Ernie's daughter-in-law died sudden and he went to live with his son to give him a bit of comfort with his company. My rheumatics got quite bad, 'specially in my hands, but I managed to do my garden and shared the vegetables with young Lizzie. It grieved me that I couldn't be a real help to her. Charlie, your Dad, was only 11 years old when he had to go to work in the pit as hod boy to his stepfather.

"By then a school had been built only half a mile away by the government. It was free and children could stay on till they were fourteen, but nobody bothered if they left early. He was the best-tempered little boy you could ever meet, a bit dreamy and quiet. The teachers didn't bother with him much but he had more brains than all of them put together. It was very hard on the little boy. He was sleeping at the foot of his sisters' bed, and often he was pushed out when they stretched their legs in their sleep. He often went to school with newspaper folded inside his boots when the soles had holes in them. And he had to fetch water from the village well before school. With only a piece of toast to keep him going, no wonder he sometimes got into trouble for napping in school.

"Being hod boy was a terrible job for a boy his age but he never grumbled. His stepfather was a miserable sort but not a bad man. I can only remember him acting wrong once. Them days the men was paid 3d a ton for all the coal they could send to the face. It was hard luck if they got on a bad seam with stone in it. One time they was on an awful seam, nearly all stone and they got nothing for that. At the end of the week your Grancher had only got 4 shillings and 3 pence wages to come.

"To make thing harder, the pit manager was very friendly with some of the town's tradesmen and let them put up stalls near the pit-head on pay-day. This way the tradesmen could get rid of the cheese too hard to sell in the shop, fish beginning to go off and other stuff that had been about too long. The men who didn't buy off these stalls were the first to be put off when work got slack.

"Your Grancher spent a precious 6 pence on cheese and some kippers. To go home with only 3 shillings and 9 pence, out of which he wanted 4 pence for his twist baccy, was more than your Grancher could face. His manhood was threatened that he could not provide for his wife and little daughters. Maddened with frustration, he gave the cheese and kippers to your Dad to take home to Granny and went into the pub at the bottom of the village.

"For a man who was not a drinker the money was enough to buy plenty of beer to dull his pain and conscience. He got home and started to take his vengeance out on your granny.

"She came into me with the little ones and he vented his temper on the furniture. Your granny understood and forgave him. I never knew him to get in a temper again, but it affected your Dad deeply. Over the years the ways in which the miners were treated turned him into what people call a socialist or some say communist. It can't be a bad thing, for if you read the Bible, the Lord himself was against the rich and the greedy and they hounded him to the cross for it.

"Your Dad had no greed in him. When he was coming up to twenty-one years old, your Granny told him the cottage they lived in was now his and he could charge them rent. He took his mam by the shoulders and told her, 'I don't want this ever mentioned again, Mother, the cottage is yours for as long as you want it.'

"It's thanks to your great-grandfather, my wench, that we have this cottage to live in. In his day, there wasn't many people living in the Forest. It was a pretty wild place, a Royal hunting ground for deer and wild boar. 'Tis said the powers that be wanted workers to fell timber from the Forest to build ships, and to be charcoal burners and work in the pits that were being sunk for the coal. To get men to settle, they offered that any man who could build a dwelling between sunrise and sunset, and have smoke coming through the chimney by then, could claim squatter's rights to it. Also he could have all the land he could fence in during the same period.

"Men and their families got together, getting stone from the quarries and timber from the Forest, and sweated their hearts out helping each other to build their homes. Of course, they weren't much, those cottages, merely one or two rooms with a fireplace, but it was a roof over their heads, and once they had them, they could build a privy down the garden and pigs' cots, and made good gardens out of their bits of land.

"It was soon after that work got so poor in the Forest pits, your Dad walked into Wales to find work in the coalfields down there. He had to get very cheap lodgings. One day a young Welsh miner, a pit butty named Will, noticed how poor the food was he brought for bait time. Will lived up the side of the mountain with his mother in a primitive farm cottage. His brothers and sisters were married except for his youngest sister, who worked as a domestic on a farm some four miles away. He asked his mother would she give lodgings to the young Forester. She agreed and your Dad moved up there. The food was plentiful if plain.

"Your Granny was a fine good-looking woman, small wonder she had been taken advantage of as a young woman and had a son. Perhaps that is why she was glad to accept marriage with a small gnome-like little man and bear him six children.

They were ill-matched in temperament, so when the children were all independent he moved along the lane on the mountain to live in a tiny cottage. Your Granny did his washing and such, and they were good friends so long as they lived apart.

"Your Dad used to go to see him and reckoned he was the most charming human being he had met. He was a wonderful drawer too, give him a pencil and a piece of paper and he could draw things so well you felt you could pick them off the paper.

"Every other Sunday, his mate's sister was given half day off to walk home. Will used to walk her back to her job. Her name was Maggie. At first she was not impressed with the pale-faced young Forester, but her hour-glass figure and air of confidence, despite the fact she wore glasses, soon had him smitten and he took over Will's job of walking her back after her Sunday afternoons off. It was a lonely walk, but very beautiful, 'specially on a summer's day.

"The little dells were tempting places to sit and Cupid have got a sharp eye for such places, so before long they was planning to get married."

CHAPTER
ELEVEN

A Big Mistake

"Whilst this was going on I was making the biggest mistake of my life. It was a poor sad life for me without my John and with your Dad away in Wales, so I took to going to Chapel a lot for comfort. Being with other people singing the lovely old hymns was a great help. I specially loved 'Rock of Ages'. I've told your Dad I want it sung at my funeral. To make things better, a new preacher came most Sundays. He was a stranger come to live not far away. His sermons were wonderful and he had such a kind gentle face he reminded me of my John. He was in his fifties and appeared to have no family.

"After Chapel, he seemed to pick me out to talk to and I was very flattered when he walked with me up the village to my home. Eventually I asked him in to a bit of supper. He was so grateful and polite. He noticed how my hands were misshapen with the arthritis and insisted on clearing the table and washing-up. I thought he was a real gentleman and a devout Christian. Loneliness blinded my judgement, for before a year was out he had persuaded me to marry him.

"I still feel ashamed when I think of myself, for I had married a foul hypocrite, a cruel fraud, a man wearing the cloak of humility and Christianity. He looked almost angelic but he should have been wearing horns and cloven feet."

"What did he do that was wicked, Auntie?"

"'Tisn't for young ears like yours, my wench, you wouldn't understand, but it made me feel bad just to be under the same roof as him, so I got his things together and threw him out with them. He pleaded and snivelled but I felt I had betrayed my John, my family, myself, and even the Almighty by being taken in by him. He threatened to commit suicide but I still wouldn't give in. He went and drowned himself in the pond not far from the church. All I hope is that he did it to pay for his sins, maybe then the Almighty might have showed him some mercy for I couldn't."

It was hard to believe that Auntie could hate anyone like that. She always took the side of people who made mistakes and spoke up to give them another chance, but Dad had already told me how she had come home from service aged 15 and thrown a nasty woman out of her cottage because she had been 'orrid to her little sisters. It was all very puzzling.

CHAPTER
TWELVE

A New Family

After a time, while I was thinking these thoughts, and Auntie was quiet and reflective, she said, "I was beginning to wonder what was the point of going on. When your Dad wrote he was going to get married and he was hoping to come back to the Forest to settle down, that bucked my spirits up no end. I was sad I couldn't give them much of a wedding present, but I offered them a home, to come to and live with me. And so they did and I got a family at last, for your Dad's been more than a son to me.

"'Tis no life if you can't share the joys and sorrows of loved ones and there have been plenty of both. Your mam and me weren't all that well-matched but we adjusted and I could never repay her for bringing you children into my life. Your sister Bess came first, well, 'tis Bess for short. Your Mam and Dad christened her Elizabeth after your Granny and me. I never saw a prettier child. she soon had us all nigh worshipping her.

"The next baby, a little girl, lived only a few hours. After her your Mam had a baby boy, Horace. He had something wrong with his heart. It was a terrible worry. When your Dad wasn't down the pit, he never let him out of his sight. Before he could crawl, he lived in your Dad's arms and would cling on with his arms round your Dad's neck whilst your Dad was doing any jobs round the house and garden. It was almost like they were joined together. If your Dad had been a kangaroo, they would never have been apart.

"Your Dad idolised him, and he was a remarkable clever toddler, talking before he was two. He always called your Dad, Daddy Charlie, but all the love in the world won't stop a child getting ill, 'specially a delicate one like Horace. He caught a cold and it turned to pneumonia. Your Dad ran the three miles to the doctor's, but the doctor wouldn't come, just gave your Dad a bottle of medicine. Poor little Horace, his weak heart wouldn't let him put up a fight. He died in your Dad's arms before the morning.

"I almost feared for your Dad's reason. You know what a gentle sort your Dad is. He'd rather shush a fly through the window than kill it. He thought the doctor might have saved Horace if he'd come. We had to beg, plead and hold on to him to stop him going to that doctor. I think he could have killed him in his grief.

"You were just a few months old at the time. With two little girls, your Dad and Mam had to pull themselves together for your sakes. I often think it's a pity the Almighty didn't make it a rule that poor people could only have a child every five years or so. You were 18 months old when your baby brother, Sydney, came along.

"We were all so thankful he was not only healthy but an outstandingly pretty child. Your Granny was always in here from next door, cuddling and playing with him and declaring he was far too pretty and good for a boy, he should have been a girl. There's an old saying 'the Lord do take the good 'uns first', and perhaps that's how it is, for before he was three years old, little Sydney died of brain fever."

I can well remember this tragedy myself, particularly the sense of dread when he was taken ill.

This time the doctor came at once and ordered him to hospital. The cottage hospital in the Forest hadn't been built at this time, so he had to go to Gloucester 20 miles away. I was aware of the shroud of misery hanging over everything, and of Mam and Granny going to get the train to Gloucester to go and see him. Dad was down the pit on evening shift. Old Auntie sat sighing in her chair by the fire. Sensing the atmosphere I sat quietly on the fender.

It had grown dark when we heard the footsteps across the yard, the door opened, and grey-faced, puffy-eyed Mam and Grannie came in. There was no need to speak.

"God bless him," said Auntie, "Him's gone to a far better place."

In the following days, when Dad wasn't at work he was in his little shed at the bottom of the garden making Sydney's coffin. Indoors he sat with his head in his hands. Old Auntie would put her hand on his shoulder. They didn't speak, but young as I was I sensed their heartbreaking concern for each other. When Sydney was brought home and laid in his coffin in the tiny downstairs front room, Auntie lifted me up to see him as she put a posy of flowers in his hands. Her tears fell on him, she was talking more to herself than me, "Oh my precious, to think you suffered so that you bit your fingers to the bare knuckles. Never mind, you be at peace now in heaven above," and she put me down and kissed him.

CHAPTER
THIRTEEN

Visiting with Auntie

Although Auntie didn't realise it, I think she sowed the seeds of a melancholia in my mind which have never really left me. Bent badly from her rheumatics by the time I was about seven years old, my shoulder acted as a second walking stick to help her laboriously hobble round the village to sit with other old neighbours, some of them living on their own. My perch was always the fender. They talked a lot about the past, often repeating themselves word for word.

Death of others and their own mortality figured largely in the talk. They saw the Almighty's hand in any trivial incident, such as a picture falling from the wall. This was seen as a portent of death, and as death was a fairly frequent happening, it strengthened their belief. It didn't seem to occur to them that the string the picture was hung by had become perished.

They believed implicitly that old Mimey who lived in an isolated cottage about a mile away was a witch. When she had caught under cover of pitch darkness Herby Anson stealing a chicken from her cote, how could she tell it was him? But she had called after him, "I know it's you, Herby Anson, and I'll put a curse on you." A few days afterward he had lost a leg in a pit accident.

When the local farmer had spoken sharply to her for going into his apple orchard to pick blackberries, hadn't his hay barn gone on fire in the middle of the afternoon, with not a soul about except him and his wife? She always encouraged the gypsies into her cottage. They must have taught her how to cast spells and make powerful brews for sick people, for she was not all bad. Without being told she had known when little Georgie Tippens was thought to be dying with a stomach complaint and had come down to the village and brought a bottle of her brew to give his mother.

Mrs Tippen was afraid to give it to him in case it was poison but afraid not to give it to him in case she evoked Mimey's wrath. She dosed Georgie with it and in a couple of days he was well again.

There could be no doubt about it, old Mimey was a witch.

Up until the age of about 60 all female neighbours were given the honorary title of

"Auntie"; after that they were all "Granny".
Granny Webb was special, not only was she 90
years old and still very clear in the head but she
had done a miracle saving her great-grandson's
twins. She was living with her great-grandson
when his wife went into a difficult first labour.
The doctor had to be fetched and he delivered
premature twin boys, both under 4 lb in weight.
He was relieved to save the mother but shook his
head about the babies and left them lying
together in a basket without any advice, giving
them no hope of survival.

Granny Webb scalded a bit of white cloth,
rolled it into a tiny tube, mixed a few grains of
sugar in boiled water with a drop of brandy,
soaked her home-made rag teats in it and
squeezed drops from it into the babies' mouths.
The doctor was astonished to find them still alive
the next morning, and dumbfounded when they
had survived a week. Of course, not only did
they get the sugar water, they had gentle hands
stroking them, tender lips kissing them and soft
voices coaxing them to live. Also, by then Granny
Webb had thought of another ploy.

They had a fountain pen in the house in which
the ink was fed into the nib by a tiny rubber
tube. Thoroughly cleansed, this tube became the
feeding bottle with a teaspoon of milk added to

the sugar water. Fed every half hour night and day, they gradually grew strong enough to suck on an ordinary bottle teat, for their mother was too ill to produce milk for them.

At last both mother and twins were doing well and Granny Webb was a village heroine. She and old Auntie praised the Almighty and gave Him all the credit.

More frequently we went to see Auntie Ginny. She laughed a lot, when she could get her breath and stop coughing. She was thin as a skeleton with longish wispy white hair and a white face. She lived in a one-up and one-down cottage. Her husband had died long ago in the asylum, but she had some wonderful daughters, all away in service and keeping her from their own meagre wages. Ginny liked a drop of gin in her tea and insisted Auntie had a spoonful in hers. Auntie always bought a currant bun off the baker for Ginny.

I took little interest in their conversation as Ginny gave me the pretty cards to look at that her daughters brought home from their jobs, Christmas cards and birthday cards their employers threw out. It was a terrible shock when Auntie told me Ginny was dead and we were going up to see her laid out. The wraithlike corpse could not be old Ginny. It looked like her but where was Ginny gone?

Far less frequently Auntie went to sit with Granny Herbert who, I sensed, she didn't like all that much, but I loved Granny Herbert's cottage. It seemed almost like a fairy house, for Granny Herbert loved pretty shiny things. She was a regular magpie, with a genius for wheedling things she fancied from their owners. Her black-leaded grate, steel fender, brass mantel rod and brass knickknacks always shone and you could see your face in them. She had mirrors with painted flowers on them and lots of dainty china ornaments and pretty pictures. The rag rugs on her floor were always free of dust.

She lived on her own and had no-one working in the pit to bring the coal-dust home on their clothing. She scrubbed her stone-flagged floor every day and marked the joins with whitening powder. I was never tired of gazing at her things.

She was six years younger than Auntie and had her eye on Auntie's pair of china dogs. Her aim when we visited was to get Auntie to promise them to her when she died and a lot of bribery went on with the cajoling, such as a piece of cake with the cup of tea. She never managed to pin Auntie down!

Now and again we went to sit with Old Ben and his dog Bess, who were inseparable. Old Ben was nearly blind but Bess acted as his sight. Bess was a great oddity, especially to the village children, for she had one brown eye and one blue one. A bachelor, Ben was retired from the pit, and Bess was the other half of his life. They lived in the tiny cottage that had belonged to his parents.

He and Auntie didn't have a lot to say to each other, and often they both dozed off, mouths agape, each side of the fire. Bess would have slept too but I kept gently poking her awake so I could look at her odd eyes.

CHAPTER
FOURTEEN

Aunt Lizzie's Hat

My adoration of old Auntie did have one reservation. Every year for my sister Bessie's birthday she made for her two pairs of drawers. They were of striped flannelette, and the legs came to the knee finished with a band of material and a frill. On my birthday a year later, in the same month of July, they were handed down to me. I didn't mind if they had a patch or two, it was the size and length that bothered me.

The drawer legs came well below my dress, for my sister was four years older than me. It brought ribald laughter from the boys and made me late for school, hanging about behind everybody else out of sight on the way there.

All was forgiven on Christmas morning when not only did old Auntie give us a shiny new penny each, she also let us have some of her precious Nestles milk to spread on our breakfast toast. Another treat we always had was when a nephew of hers came once a year to see her. She had once lent him some money, which he duly paid back, but he had also taken out an insurance policy on her life.

He was the opposite of my Dad, a sharp mercenary type, ready to take advantage of anyone for a bargain. Auntie's longevity was, she reckoned, a source of irritation to him. She considered he only came in the hope she was on her last legs, as he always only brought her a packet of humbugs and a few apples from the tree in his garden. She was costing him money and it pleased her to put on a false impression of "feeling much better than last year".

"It do aggravate him so," she would chuckle when he left.

Every Sunday thereafter, while they lasted we were given a humbug each and a portion of an apple. Unfortunately, they all tasted strongly of camphor, for Auntie kept them in the drawer with her laying-out clothes well-sprinkled with moth-balls.

Even when her hands were cruelly misshapen with arthritis and she could no longer manage to use her treadle-sewing machine, she still tried to do the family mending. Turning a sheet sides to middle on one occasion, she sewed her navy spotted apron to the mended sheet.

When annoyed, she always sent the offending object or person to Halifax — I don't know what Halifax had done to deserve it. The object that was despatched to Halifax the most was a neighbour's cat. It got into Auntie's bedroom through the window and she was convinced it brought the fleas that plagued her at night, making her itch where her rheumaticky old fingers couldn't reach. Poor thanks for any little scraps she could put out for the poor beast.

Apart from her laying-out clothes and the previously mentioned five guineas to give her a decent funeral, old Auntie had another "hair" loom. It was a hat of black straw with a wide brim, bought many years ago for John's funeral. Then it had been trimmed with black ribbon bows. Over the years, as a sort of homage to John, she had added every bit of black trimming that came her way: a small ostrich feather, a Mynah bird, a bunch of black cherries, some bits of jet, draped black net and some sprays of black flowers. It was very heavy.

By the time she wore it for the last time, when she managed to go to Chapel for Anniversary Day, her frail old neck could hardly balance it.

It had taken years and God knows what sacrifices for our village to have the sturdy little chapel built in the middle of the village. Every summer, on the Sunday nearest the date on which it was finished, was held Anniversary Day. It was a most important day in the village's calendar, when the chapel and its activities were the main centre of social intercourse. It gave those with a bit of finery a chance to show it off, a chance for mothers (not many men were chapel-goers) to watch proudly as their children recited sanctimonious poems and sang solos such as

> Jesus loves me, that I know
> 'cos the Bible tells me so

and

> Jesus makes us shine with a clear pure light
> Like a little candle burning in the night.

All the little girls were supposed to be dressed in white. Many couldn't manage it and there was little true Christian feeling between the show-offs with their lace and ribbon-trimmed white finery and those of us who sat at the back of the stage in whatever colour respectable clothes that our Mams could rustle up.

When she got home that day, I was given the honour of putting it on her bed ready for when she could wrap it up in voluminous amounts of paper in a cardboard box under her bed. The trial of getting to the Chapel, to witness me trying the patience of the congregation with a long sanctimonious poem because it was Anniversary Day, and back had tired her out.

After tea she decided to go to bed for a rest. Some neighbours had just come in and soon we were in full flow of gossip about the congregation's dress and behaviour. After about 15 minutes Auntie's door opened. There she stood, a very forlorn figure with a large decrepit object hanging in her hand — it was her hat!

Poor Auntie, she was in tears as she wailed "Oh me 'at, me 'at. I've ruined it, serve me right. I reckon it's the hand o' the Almighty punishin' me for being so cruel to the cat, for I forgot me 'at had been put on the bed, and I mistook it for that dratted black cat. I walloped it wi' me walkin' stick. When the cheeky varmint took no notice, I walloped it some more. Then I felt sorry and went to stroke it, an' I realised it was me 'at. 'Tis them cataracts on me eyes. I wish they was in Halifax, for I have such a job to see!"

We all knew my big sister Bess was a real clever clogs. She studied the battered hat and assured Auntie she would make it wearable again. Up till then Auntie had not decided who should be the fortunate inheritor of her hat and now she made up her mind.

"Right, my wench, if you do, it shall be yours when I be gone."

Perhaps it was a good job she couldn't see the expression on Bessie's face at this magnificent gesture!

★　★　★

Thereafter the hat remained in the box under the bed as to walk the 300 yards to Chapel had become a bigger undertaking than going to America all those years ago.

CHAPTER
FIFTEEN

The End Comes

Auntie started to stir a little in the bed.

"Help me sit up, my wench, the strength be gone right out o' me."

Poor Auntie, to be so stiff and helpless having been so active all her life. If only it was time for the nettles to be growing, between the edge of the forest and the village. The space was filled with areas of grass tumps, large shallow holes for rubbish tips, interspersed in season with beds of nettles. Auntie liked to boil up saucepans of nettles to eat.

They were a nuisance to pick as we didn't have such a luxury as a pair of gloves in our house, but my sister Bess would try and pick them firmly by the bottom of the stem. Auntie didn't mind how they stung her as she prepared them for cooking, for she reckoned the stings as well as the cooked nettles helped to ease her rheumatism.

As I was trying to make her comfortable, Dad came in from his long walk to the hospital to see

Mam, who was now improving, and he sat down to keep Auntie company. Bess was making them a cup of tea so I went out to play.

The next day, when I got home from school, old Auntie's chair by the fireside was empty. Bess said, "'er ent very well today, felt too tired to get up, said 'er'd 'ave a rest. You take 'er tea in."

Having been in service and learnt fancy ways, Bess had done Auntie some wafer-thin bread and butter cut in little squares, with a nice hot strong sweet cup of tea. It was still quite a struggle for her to get it down, but after she said "My, my, tell Bess that were lovely, made me fell like a real lady."

The effort to eat made her nod off. When eventually she opened her eyes again, she sat up on her own and started to talk to people I couldn't see. I still sat there, thinking that when they had gone she would be lonely, but she dozed off again and was still sleeping when Dad came back from his nightly walk to the hospital.

In the morning, when I took Auntie her cup of tea before I went to school, I couldn't rouse her enough to sit up and take her tea.

"I be awful tired, my wench, I'll drink it later on." The words came slowly and with effort. I shouted out to Bess to take Auntie some tea later on as she was too tired to drink this one and hurried off to school.

When I got home again, old Auntie was dead. It seemed too awful a burden for my thirteen year old heart and mind to accept. How could home be home without Auntie there? With no wrinkled, arthritically deformed old hand lifted to calm us all down in our little family differences. Mortality, this black unspeakable bottomless hole going into nothingness, it crippled my mind.

★ ★ ★

Mother was not well enough to come home for the funeral. Chairs were put outside the garden gate to rest the coffin on whilst our neighbours and friends gathered round to sing *Abide With Me* as she had wanted, then Father and some male neighbours lifted it onto their shoulders for the two-mile walk to church, to see her "put tidy into her grave".

Trying not to let her go, I kept remembering all I could about her. I remembered, though I couldn't recall by what means, the time she took us on an outing to Gloucester to see a jam factory. All I really recall of the day (I was about two and a half years old) was the sight of some men standing on a large platform in front of huge boilers of jam, stirring them with wooden spoons as big as garden spades. The platforms meant the men were above the level of the jam boilers and old Auntie expressed the worry that, working in the intense heat, a man might faint and topple in. I think the name of the factory was Stephen's Jam.

The First World War was still raging then and it was about that time rumours abounded of the atrocities committed by German soldiers. I could understand what was being said but couldn't express any thoughts of my own. The words Kaiser and German filled me with dread. I remember I was on my usual perch, sitting on the corner of the steel fender, when I heard Mam say, "Them Germans soldiers do put babies on the end o' bayonets and do what they will with the mothers."

"Doosn't worry, Maggie," comforted old Auntie, "If ever that Kaiser and his soldiers do land in England, I'll gather some Deadly Nightshade and make some poison. We'll give it the little 'uns first, and when they be dead we'll take it ourselves."

Dad came in as they were talking, and they expressed their fears to him. He exploded with fury, "'Tis nothin' but a wicked lot o' lies! The

German men be the same as we men. Like us they 'ave swallowed all the propaganda put into their 'eads by the big powers that do rule us all. 'Tis to keep the power and wealth that is in this world for themselves that countries do fight each other, and the people do swallow it all, put on uniforms and go murderin' each other by the thousands. The hate is whipped up by such tales as you two 'ave listened to. No doubt German women is swallowin' the same tales 'bout we Englishmen!"

Mam and old Auntie seemed to be comforted by Dad's word. As for me I now felt neither the Kaiser nor the Germans could get past him to harm us.

POSTSCRIPT

Now tottering into my 88th year, crippled with osteoarthritis as you were, I often think of you, Auntie. Like you, I can't remember from one minute to the next where I have put my specs or walking stick, but the early years are crystal-clear. I can understand the heights of your happiness and the depths of your despair. The bereavement of a loved one is like the rape of the spirit and the tortured pleas of "why?" bring no answer.

How I wish I had your simple faith in a divine Almighty, making mortality something to be welcomed. Your beloved nephew Charlie, my Dad, was killed in the mine at the age of 57, and the sun has never shone in its full glory for me ever since. Then, after nearly 60 years of marriage, I woke in the early hours to find my husband dead beside me, so I know the hell of loneliness you endured when you lost Uncle John Webb. Despite the privilege and blessings

(and worries) of having four fine children —
three boys and one girl, who have given me 10
grandchildren and six great-grandchildren — I
feel unutterably sad.

Now, too immobile for activity, I have
over-much time to ponder on the imponderables
— I marvel at this planet orbiting in space every
twenty-four hours, with a fire burning in its belly,
with its myriad of life-forms varying from the
microscopic too small for the eye to see to the
whale and the elephant, and breathtaking
varieties of flora, and with its billions of tons of
trash. For there can be no positive without its
negative, evil and decay walk with goodness and
beauty. The magnitude of creation reduces the
posturings and egotism of the human race to
size.

How brief seems our lifetime — how we long
for immortality. I think the privilege of
reproduction is the answer nature gave us. When
the rose that blooms in ethereal beauty drops its
petals, it is gone for good. But its beauty is
recreated the next year when there is a new bud
that will expand and show to the world that there
is still life to be found.

The great question remains for mankind: to
find an identity in the universe which has so
much diversity. Life has changed dramatically by

human application of cleverness and inventiveness, Auntie, but all the clever machines do not replace the essence of humanity. We are better off in material terms, but far worse off in human ones.

Remember when you stood with us outside the cottage door pointing out the face of the man in the moon? Man has become so clever, Auntie, he has invented the means to travel the millions of miles to land on the moon. It has no life there, just an arid surface of huge pot holes, and on the way there was no Heaven or angels floating about.

A car is no longer a novelty; almost every home in Britain has at least one, just as practically every home has at least one miniature cinema, with a choice of many programmes on every subject available at the touch of a button, day and night. The hearth is no longer the centrepiece of the home — many do not even have one.

Heat for cooking, hot water, light and warmth now come from gas, electricity and oil, mostly piped from their various sources under the ground, all to be switched on indoors at a finger's touch. A telephone is normal to any household; there are minute mobile ones weighing a couple of ounces which can be carried in a pocket so that at any time we can make instant contact with other users.

I could go on and on, Auntie, about the conveniencies and luxuries now commonplace to daily life. But, of course, there is a price: wives and mothers must go out to work to pay for them. What has become extremely scarce is time for each other and the need for each other's help. Who wants their old folk sat in the corner reminiscing, or the prattle of the children, when the television is a more entertaining and trouble-free attraction. Old people can be put in homes where they can watch the TV all day and children can be put in front of it when mothers come home from work and have no time to sit with them.

It has become the monstrous robot guest, dominating our lives, force-feeding our minds like turkeys are force fed for Christmas. Life is becoming an indigestible turmoil, with a huge undercurrent wave of depression. We are losing each other in the paraphernalia of progress. No matter. Time, that power we cannot feel, hear, touch, taste, smell or see, pushes us all inexorably into "that bourn from which no traveller returns". Now nearing that journey, I wonder if, as Shakespeare wrote, "Life is a tale told by an idiot, full of sound and fury, signifying nothing".

Oh Auntie, I wish I was a little girl again with your comforting hand on my head.

ISIS publish a wide range of books in large print, from fiction to biography. Any suggestions for books you would like to see in large print or audio are always welcome. Please send to the Editorial department at:

ISIS Publishing Ltd.
7 Centremead
Osney Mead
Oxford OX2 0ES
(01865) 250 333

A full list of titles is available free of charge from:
Ulverscroft large print books

(UK)
The Green
Bradgate Road, Anstey
Leicester LE7 7FU
Tel: (0116) 236 4325

(Australia)
P.O Box 953
Crows Nest
NSW 1585
Tel: (02) 9436 2622

(USA)
1881 Ridge Road
P.O Box 1230, West Seneca,
N.Y. 14224-1230
Tel: (716) 674 4270

(Canada)
P.O Box 80038
Burlington
Ontario L7L 6B1
Tel: (905) 637 8734

(New Zealand)
P.O Box 456
Feilding
Tel: (06) 323 6828

Details of **ISIS** complete and unabridged audio books are also available from these offices. Alternatively, contact your local library for details of their collection of **ISIS** large print and unabridged audio books.

f. Stanford march 16 2015